CCSS Genre **Folktale**

 Essential Question
What makes different animals unique?

KING
OF THE BIRDS

A Mayan Folktale

retold by Karen Alexander • illustrated by Linda Bittner

Chapter 1
THE GATHERING

The forest was full of birds. Birds sat on the branches. Some birds looked for insects to eat. Some birds made nests. All day long, the birds squabbled, or argued.

Hawk looked around the forest in dismay. He had ruled the birds for many years, but he was old and tired of the birds fighting. Hawk told the birds to choose a new king.

tree trunk

hawk

branch

The birds had a meeting to choose a new king. Each bird secretly wanted to be king.

Mockingbird thought she should be king because she had a splendid voice. Mockingbird sang her heart out. Mockingbird sang the songs of crickets, frogs, and the other birds.

The birds were very impressed. They thought that maybe Mockingbird should be king.

In Other Words put in a lot of effort. En español, *sang her heart out* quiere decir *cantó con toda su corazón.*

mockingbird

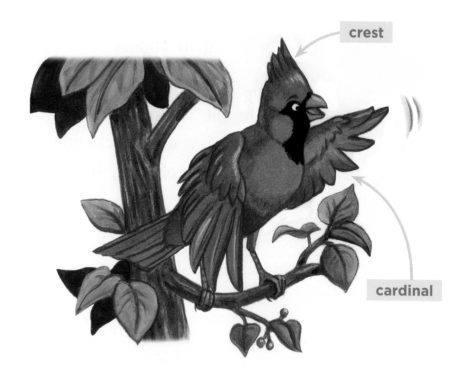

crest

cardinal

Then Cardinal <u>strutted</u> in front of the birds. He showed off his wonderful red feathers. Cardinal made the crest on his head stand up.

The birds were amazed by Cardinal's beautiful scarlet feathers and his strong beak. The birds thought that maybe Cardinal should be king.

Language Detective	<u>Strutted</u> is an action verb. Find another action verb on this page.

Next, Turkey offered herself as king. Turkey puffed up her chest. Turkey said that she was big and strong, so she could keep the peace and stop fights. Turkey said she was watchful, so she would protect the birds from danger.

The birds liked what Turkey said. They thought that maybe Turkey should be king.

quetzal

6

All types of birds explained why they should be king. There were loud birds and quiet birds and boastful birds and shy birds. As each bird spoke, the other birds thought that maybe this was the bird that should be king.

But Quetzal did not speak. The other birds looked at Quetzal in disbelief. Quetzal was usually confident and ambitious.

STOP AND CHECK

Why did the birds have a meeting?

Chapter 2

QUETZAL FOR KING!

Quetzal had a problem. He was clever and smart. Quetzal knew he would be a good king, but his feathers were not colorful. Then Quetzal thought of Roadrunner. Roadrunner had fabulous, colorful feathers.

feathers

Quetzal talked to Roadrunner. Quetzal said that he would make the best king, but he needed colorful feathers to be king. Quetzal told Roadrunner that she had splendid feathers.

Quetzal tried to convince Roadrunner to lend her feathers to Quetzal. In return, Quetzal promised to share all the riches of being king with Roadrunner.

Roadrunner was not happy with the idea. Roadrunner liked her feathers. She would be cold without her feathers. But it wasn't long before Roadrunner gave the feathers to Quetzal.

Quetzal added Roadrunner's feathers to his own feathers. He did not give any of his feathers to Roadrunner.

Roadrunner's feathers

quetzal

Quetzal went to the meeting of the birds. He looked magnificent. Quetzal was a very good speaker. Soon, Quetzal had convinced the birds to choose him as the new king.

STOP AND CHECK

In what ways did Quetzal show he was clever?

Chapter 3

ROADRUNNER BETRAYED

Quetzal was a very busy king. He forgot his promise to Roadrunner.

The other birds realized that they had not seen Roadrunner. The birds <u>searched</u> for her.

Language Detective	<u>Searched</u> is an action verb. Find another action verb on this page.

At last, the birds found Roadrunner. Roadrunner was cold and hungry. She had been hiding because she had no feathers.

The birds gave food to Roadrunner. Each bird gave Roadrunner some feathers to keep her warm.

food

Roadrunner got well again. However, she was sad because she did not have her beautiful feathers. Roadrunner's new feathers were different colors and shapes. She looked strange. She wanted to have her own feathers.

> **In Other Words** stopped being cold and hungry. En español, *got well* quiere decir *se mejoró*.

roadrunner

road

Roadrunner waited for Quetzal to return her colorful feathers. But Quetzal did not return them. Even today, Roadrunner races around. She is searching for Quetzal.

STOP AND CHECK

What did the other birds do when they found Roadrunner?

Respond to Reading

Summarize

Use important details to summarize *King of the Birds*. Your graphic organizer may help you.

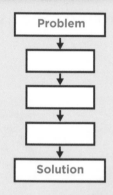

Problem
↓
↓
↓
Solution

Text Evidence

1. How do you know *King of the Birds* is a folktale? GENRE

2. What problem does Quetzal have? How does he solve the problem? PROBLEM AND SOLUTION

3. Find the word *scarlet* on page 4. What nearby word helps you figure out what *scarlet* means? SYNONYMS

4. Write to describe Hawk's problem and the solution he found. WRITE ABOUT READING

Compare Texts
Read about the unique quetzal.

THE REAL QUETZAL

Quetzals live in rain forests in Central America. Male quetzals have beautiful, bright feathers and a long green tail. A male quetzal's body is about 15 inches long. The tail can grow to about 3 feet.

Quetzals belong to a family of birds that has a unique feature. The two inner toes face backward, and the two outer toes face forward. This feature helps the birds to perch on the branches of trees but makes it difficult for the birds to walk.

Bird Feet	
the foot of most birds	the foot of a quetzal
Y	X

17

People have admired quetzals for thousands of years. Quetzals were important in Mayan culture. Mayan rulers decorated their clothes with quetzal feathers. The Mayans also traded quetzal feathers. The male's green tail feathers were more valuable than gold. For this reason, quetzals were a sign of wealth.

It is easier to hear quetzals than to see them. Quetzals hide among the green leaves of the forest.

Quetzals use their beaks to hollow out a rotting tree. Then they build a nest.

Today, quetzals are endangered. One reason is that people hunt quetzals for their feathers. Another reason is that people are destroying the rain forests, where quetzals live. However, in some countries, quetzals are now protected.

Make Connections

How does *The Real Quetzal* help you understand what makes an animal unique? ESSENTIAL QUESTION

Does the description of the quetzal in *The Real Quetzal* help you understand the quetzal in *King of the Birds*? TEXT TO TEXT

Focus on Genre

Folktale *King of the Birds* is a folktale. A folktale is a story that is passed down by storytellers. Each person who tells the story changes it a little. Folktales often describe animals as if they were people. Some folktales try to teach us a lesson.

Read and Find Many folktales have animals that act like humans. The animals can be greedy or vain. The events that happen in a folktale could not happen in real life. For example, in *King of the Birds*, Roadrunner lends her feathers to Quetzal. This could not really happen. Folktales teach us about human nature and give us rules on how we should behave. These rules are called morals.

Your Turn

With a partner, choose one event from *King of the Birds* and discuss how you would change it. Write sentences to describe the change you made to the story. Then, take turns with your partner to tell the new story.